PREFACE

Timed to coincide with the nineteenth *John Moores Open National Painting Competition* and *Visionfest*, Liverpool's annual festival of the visual arts, *Making It* is a celebration of contemporary art, its practitioners and its audience. The exhibiting artists have all been asked to make new work specially for the exhibition, and the resulting installations, paintings and sculptures offer a series of different invitations and challenges to visitors to the Gallery.

Tate Gallery Liverpool was established to show the national Collection of modern art, and its programme of temporary exhibitions complements and extends the scope of the Collection. In this context, the Gallery is pleased to show the work of this group of young British artists, whose diversity of practice hints at the tremendous creativity within the visual arts in this country at the moment.

Much of the work in this exhibition has been made using methods and materials which extend conventional notions of art practice. It has brought artists into contact with several firms working in the North West and elsewhere, whose help and advice has been invaluable. We are indebted to Bacofoil, Benson Signs and Tate & Lyle for their expertise and material support. We are grateful to the people who work in Liverpool's Liver Building for their contributions to *Looking Both Ways* and we thank our sponsor, Royal Liver Assurance.

Nicholas Serota

Director, Tate Gallery

Lewis Biggs

Curator, Tate Gallery Liverpool

SPONSORS FOREWORD

In December 1994 Royal Liver Assurance was approached by the Curator of the Tate Gallery Liverpool, Lewis Biggs, requesting our support for a new and exciting exhibition created by 'Those Environmental Artists'. The subject of the exhibition was to be the Royal Liver Building, our prestigious Head Office.

The Royal Liver Building was opened in 1911 and to this day, remains the centre of our life and endowment assurance, personal pensions, investment and tax exempt savings operation which extends throughout the whole of the United Kingdom and the Republic of Ireland.

We at Royal Liver are justly proud of our famous Head Office, which symbolises our attitude to our business and our customers which is one of trustworthiness, stability and security. Above all, our building is a symbol of Merseyside and all that this great City represents. Royal Liver Assurance is delighted to support the exceptional work of these talented individuals and contribute to our local arts community.

Michael Kelly

Marketing Director, Royal Liver Assurance

ROYAL
LIVER
ASSURANCE

Paring Scheme Award

Royal Liver Assurance is an award winner under the 'Pairing Scheme', (the National Heritage Arts Sponsorship Scheme) for its support of *Looking Both Ways* at Tate Gallery Liverpool.

INTRODUCTION

JANET HODGSON

SARAH RAINE

JAMES RIELLY

PADRAIG TIMONEY

DAPHNE WRIGHT

TEA

Making It is an exhibition about various ways of making art. It considers how artists make art, and how museums, galleries and their visitors contribute to that making. If being an artist is essentially about process, then being a viewer is about participation: art, through its materials and its meanings, extends an invitation to its audience. The works were made specially for the Gallery, and are the result of interaction between the artist, the space available and the aims of the exhibition. The individual artists are united by this rather than by any similarity of practice: the exhibition is concerned primarily with diversity.

Some of the artists engage directly with Tate Gallery Liverpool and with the theme of the exhibition, while others approach it more obliquely. Janet Hodgson's installation *White Cube, Black Square* takes on the Gallery's past as a bonded warehouse used to store luxury goods such as sugar. It invites the viewer to eavesdrop on, and join in with, a dialogue between art work and art gallery. Sarah Raine's *Splanchnology* entices the viewer inside the art object, using each viewing body as part of the installation. Daphne Wright's *Lot's Wife* calls out from hidden speakers. These three installations use the processes of their making to engage the viewer in the kind of active looking which is a form of remaking, and this is complemented by the wall-based work. James Rielly's paintings are meditations on visual acceptance and the construction of identity. Padraig Timoney operates in the gap between process and the processed, making work which uses the viewer to keep it alive after the artist has completed it.

TEA's installation *Looking Both Ways* will not be completed until the exhibition is over. 'Those Environmental Artists' have used this exhibition as an opportunity to conduct an investigation into the Royal Liver Building, one of Liverpool's most famous landmarks. The artists turn the building inside out, soliciting impressions of it from its inhabitants, its admirers and visitors to *Making It.* The role of both the artist and the viewer in the making of an art work is here explicit and on show: the viewer is asked to contribute to the work, and TEA are in the Gallery every Saturday, adding these contributions to the installation.

This catalogue seeks to extend the relationship between artist and viewer established in the exhibition. The texts have been written following conversations with the artists, and present some of the themes and ideas around which the works were made and through which they may be approached.

Fiona Bradley
Exhibition Curator

White Cube, Black Square is made from white sugar and molasses, opposite ends of the process by which cane sugar is refined in this country. The white cube is made from bricks of granulated sugar, which was dissolved in water, heated and then poured into wood and wire moulds. The black square is a tray of the same dimensions as the base of the cube, into which molasses dribbles gently. The molasses is evidence of what the sugar has lost: if you mixed the white cube with the black square you would end up with what originally arrived in the sugar factory - raw, dirty, but perfectly edible brown sugar. The refining process simply washes out the 'impurities' which become molasses.

White Cube, Black Square literalises some of the metaphors and raises some of the issues to do with art, sugar, the Tate, taste, luxury and necessity in 1990s Britain. A sugar cube made from sugar bricks, it connects Tate Gallery Liverpool's present function back to its origins in the bequest to the nation of Henry Tate's collection of the modern art of his day. Henry Tate, of Tate & Lyle, initially a Liverpool company with a major refinery in the city until 1981, made his fortune from sugar which was famous for its superior quality and purity. The building which houses Tate Gallery Liverpool is an old bonded warehouse which was originally used for storing, among other things, imported raw sugar. In building a sugar cube out of sugar bricks exactly the same size as the bricks of the Tate, the artist alludes to the history of the space. Art gallery and art object are both built from sugar - either metaphorically or literally.

Bricks *at* the Tate, as opposed to the bricks *of* the Tate, have a somewhat different history. The Tate Gallery is associated in many people's minds with Carl Andre's *Equivalent VIII* of 1966, popularly known as 'The Bricks'. This regular arrangement of firebricks is, although now almost thirty years old, still synonymous with all that some people do not like, and do not understand, about modern and contemporary art. Hodgson's sugar cube plays with this: made from similar units, *White Cube, Black Square* nods at the minimalism out of which André's work came, while also questioning the place and value of art in modern society. The white cube is also a 'white cube', the phrase often used to describe the visually neutral spaces in which much contemporary art is shown. The Tate has made a white cube out of a bonded warehouse: is there a relationship between its current and its former role in the community? The artist proposes a link between art and sugar: both are 'refined' products, and have to do with taste in either its sensory or its aesthetic sense.

While *White Cube, Black Square* may have something of the look of minimalist art, it is made from materials, and using methods, which have more to do with cooking. Minimalist art materials are self-referential, while the sugar and molasses of *White Cube, Black Square* suggest possibilities beyond the immediate form of the work. Hodgson thinks that, though physically extremely hard work, the repetitive labour which went into the making of this work connects it to traditionally female activities such as cooking, knitting and weaving: unit-based, additive processes initially scaled to the body but extending beyond it. There is a coherence to the manufacture of this sculpture which keeps it in the

White Cube, Black Sq[illegible]95
Granulated sugar, royal icing,
steel, molasses, pump
2033 x 2033mm x 2033mm;
2033 x 2033mm

JANET HODGSON

BIOGRAPHY

1960	Born Bolton, Lancashire
1978 - 1979	Lincoln College of Art
1979 - 1982	Studied Theatre Design, Wimbledon School of Art

Lives and works in Liverpool

COMMISSIONS

1990	*The Boat,* Birkenhead Park, Merseyside
	Waterfall, The Riverside, Stockton-on-Tees
	The House, Bitts Park, Carlisle
1991	*Untitled*, Dovecot Arts Centre, Stockton-on-Tees
	Saltworks, Albert Dock, Liverpool
	Parthenon II, Holyrood Park, Edinburgh
1992	*Arrivals*, Settle Market Place, North Yorkshire (with Peter Hatton)
	H_2O, Brindley Place, Birmingham (with Peter Hatton)
1993	*Liquid Matter*, Serpentine Gallery, London (with Peter Hatton)
	Watershed, Queen Elizabeth Hall, London (with Peter Hatton)
	Piltdown Bungalow, Uppermill, Yorkshire
1994	*I Must Learn To Know My Place,* Bluecoat Gallery, Liverpool
	Project Proposal, Pier Head, Liverpool

GROUP EXHIBITIONS

1992	*A Pool of Signs II*, Bluecoat Gallery, Liverpool
1993	Manchester Airport Terminal Two
1995	*Making It: Process and Participation*, Tate Gallery Liverpool

domain of the feminine and the home. Although the bricks were laid by a professional bricklayer, the 'mortar' is royal icing. Whereas the bricklayer suggested using a chemical plasticiser to keep the mixture malleable, the artist considered glycerine. In the same way, when she thought she might need an accelerator to speed up the setting of the sugar bricks, it was egg white which came to mind rather than the chemicals used in other, more common art practices, such as bronze casting.

The white cube may perhaps be understood to be 'female' and the black square 'male': 'sugar and spice and all things nice' faces 'slugs and snails and puppy dogs' tails'. The stream of molasses makes a wriggling worm in the centre of the tray, and we know that it is made from all the 'nasty' things extracted from sugar. The cube is not 'sweet', however: Hodgson avoids the literalisation of that metaphor. Sugar mice are sweet, but the cube is bold and monolithic, resisting, even with its royal icing mortar, overtones of cuteness and of gingerbread houses.

The cube remains a cube; blunt and somewhat ungainly, but twinkling with seductive possibility. Cooking to the last, the artist's intention was to 'boil down' the concept so that its simple but associatively rich ingredients could speak for themselves. The work offers meaning in sets of dyadic pairs of which female/male is only one. Art/non-art is another, so is useful/useless, pure/impure, white/black.

The work was made for Liverpool, and one axis of approach offered by the cube and the square refers also to the history of this city as one of the major trading cities of the British Empire. The slave trade and slavery had both been abolished in the Empire before the Albert Dock was built, but Liverpool is invariably referred to as a city 'built on slavery'. *White Cube, Black Square*, a work made from both pure, white sugar and the black molasses which is its exact opposite in terms of implied value, inevitably speaks of this.

Ultimately, the cube and its square maintain their own metaphor: their several sides are parallel so that the viewer can come at them from different angles, at different times, without any one approach dominating. The viewer, entranced by the sheen of the molasses as well as by the twinkle of the sugar, is invited into a complex visual, cultural and historical game.

White Cube, Black Square is generously supported by Tate & Lyle

In addition, the artist thanks Liverpool John Moores University, Appledore Lighting, Albany Pumps, Chris Shannon, Sam Smith, Jim Gallagher, Duncan Curtis and David Mabb.

Splanchnology is an interesting word. It sounds onomatopoeic even before you know what it means. Both attractive and repellent, it has possibilities for meaning which are extended rather than curtailed by its actual meaning: the study of viscera, of intestines, of entrails. It is a word which is of the body but which seems to have possibilities outside it - entrails, after all, have been used to predict the future.

As with the word, so with the work it describes. Sarah Raine's installation is charged with an ambivalence which begins in the particularity of the materials used - red velvet, red pigment, human hair - and extends into a variety of possible meanings for the art they have been used to make.

The smaller, wall-based part of the installation derives from a series of works which Raine has made on the theme of the plaque. She sees it as 'some kind of trophy'. It looks immaculate, complete, a cluster of red protuberances nestling in a mound of hair. A body part? An organ? Clearly an orifice of some kind. The viewer is held at arm's length by it, external to it, invited to look, but not to touch. Indeed, seductive though the colour is, there is also something threatening about the redness of those small forms.

The plaque, fixed to the wall, also shoots or points out from it towards the work's larger element. This is another orifice; this time a room, open and inviting. The cluster of protuberances is now hair-clad, and protected by red velvet upholstery. Equally immaculate, this element seems only to be complete when the viewer is inside - rooms are meant to be inhabited. Fended off from the plaque, the viewer is drawn into the room, to consider both its own ambivalence and the contradictory relationship it has with its opposite number. The protuberances offer a starting point from which to consider the work. Those in the room point at the viewer and might perhaps be read as 'male' to the plaque's 'female', especially when we look out at the plaque and, in the distance, see only the deceptive vulnerability and perhaps femininity of its red centre. Yet if we remember that this centre is filled with protuberances of its own, we may notice that these would in fact fit into the hollow interiors of the cone shapes which are currently surrounding and threatening us, thus reversing the male/female possibility. Once we have noticed this, other details crowd in to reinforce the ambiguity: we have entered the room - does this also make it a 'female' space? The plaque, poised so innocently opposite the room, now seems ready to leap towards it. The oppositions will not stay still.

All this ambivalence is intentional. The artist's mother is a physiotherapist: Sarah Raine grew up familiar with the vocabulary of the body, and tends to make work which uses it. In the case of *Splanchnology*, this is determined by process, shape and materials. Trained in textiles, the artist is responsive to the dictates of materials. She picks up shapes and textures which respond to and help articulate pre-existing visual ideas. Here, both velvet and hair are rich in associations. Both address the body, but from an angle that allows the work to be of it but not simply or literally about it.

The work's first point of contact with the body is the repetitive physical labour which was involved in making it and is echoed in the physical participation expected of the viewer. The cones and other protuberances are individually cast; the hair cut, gathered, sorted, sprinkled and set; the velvet stretched and the buttons pushed in painstakingly one by one. The upholstery speaks of the body by association: upholstered objects - chairs, bed-heads, sofas, coffins - traditionally contain and support the body,

Splanchnology 1995
Human hair, plaster,
pigment, velvet.
diameter: 2850mm, height 2440mm
diameter: 1190mm, depth 460mm

SARAH RAINE

BIOGRAPHY

1967	Born in London
1986 - 1989	Studied Printed Textiles, Liverpool Polytechnic
1993	Residency at Walker Art Gallery, Liverpool
1993	Residency at Oldham Art Gallery
1994	Residency at Oviedo, Spain

Lives and works in Liverpool

SOLO EXHIBITIONS

1993	*Lesser Gods*, Waterstones, Liverpool
	Art Afloat, Mersey Ferries, Liverpool
	Pink Is for Girls, Off Stage, Liverpool
1994	*Nice, Not Nice*, Arena House, Liverpool

SELECTED GROUP EXHIBITIONS

1989	*Tricel*, The Design Centre, London, Glasgow City Museum
	Surtex Trade Centre, New York
1991	*New Waves, Changing Depths*, Maritime Museum, Liverpool
	Earthbound, Young Unknowns Gallery, London
1992	*Room To Manoeuvre*, The Grand Hall, Liverpool
	The Bottom Drawer, Gill Gallery, London; F Stop Gallery, Bath; Forty Hall Museum, London; Plymouth City Art Gallery
1993	*The Arena Show*, Art Shed, Liverpool
	Young Professional Artists - North West, Castlefield Gallery, Manchester; Oriel Gallery, Theatre Clywd, Wales; Wrexham Art Gallery; Oviedo, Aviles and Gijon, Spain
1994	*Souvenir*, Paraiso Gallery, Spain
	Signification, Albert Dock, Liverpool
	Ainscough Gallery, Liverpool
	Liverpool meets Melbourne, Grand Central Gallery, Australia
1995	*All Enquiries*, Skillion Centre, Liverpool
	Making It: Process and Participation, Tate Gallery Liverpool

gathering over time an impression of it. The hair is literally of the body - cut and gathered in a hairdresser's salon.

These materials are familiar. Or perhaps, in the context of the Gallery, they are secretly familiar, the stuff of the uncanny. The uncanny is that order of things which are at once intimately known and newly encountered - things out of place, disjointed and dismembered. The hair makes this clearest. On our heads it is unremarkable; severed, it may become an object of disgust - several people were repelled by the piles of hair on the artist's studio floor as she began to work. The artist, initially attracted to the ambivalent qualities of hair as a material for art, exploits it to extend the meaning of the work. The unease which the hair inspires forces us to look for alternative meanings for it. Hair, for instance, is said to keep growing after death and the artist has described her upholstered room as 'part massage parlour, part funeral parlour'. However, there are also hair-like structures within the body, and perhaps the orifices or vessels of this installation could also be sexually innocent noses, throats and lungs.

Ultimately the hair, the velvet of the upholstery, and the redness of both velvet and pigment, are overdetermined, in the Freudian sense of being multiply symbolic. They, like the 'splanchnology' of the work's title, have potential for associative meaning way beyond their function or their originally intended role in this particular art work. Placed in the Gallery, forming the ambivalently paired shapes of this installation, they ask the viewer to do some of the work. Enticed into the artist's sumptuously upholstered room, the viewer is invited to find a conceptual as well as a formal route for their body into the work.

The artist thanks Tracey Brown for her help with the installation.

James Rielly introduces the viewer to a series of individuals organised into an extended family group: mother, father, two young children, one older child and one additional, rather more ambivalent, adult figure. The figures are painted on a blank, white background, against which they stand out with simple clarity. They have a quietness about them which is at odds with the startling incongruity of their composition, and a deadpan humour which sits uneasily alongside the themes they explore.

The paintings make a strongly physical impact. They are all large, and their consistently pale colours vibrate with a quiet intensity which comes from the green base colour with which the artist starts work. The scale of the images, and the unity of their presentation in terms of style and colour, enables them to interact with the space of the Gallery and with the audience that shares that space with them.

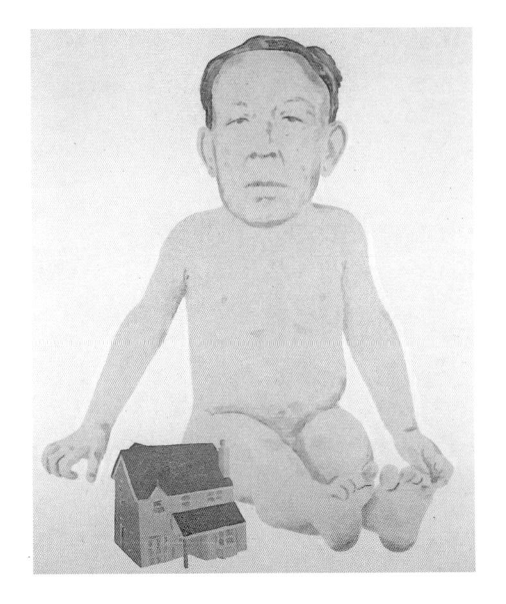

Much of the looking that these images invite is comparative. Their scale dominates the viewer, leading to an immediate comparison between painting and person. Their identity as a family group is dependent on comparison: they are a family because of the similarities, and the differences, between them. They are defined in relation to one another by both artist and viewer. *Woman* is a mother because the young children could be her children. *Man* becomes, through his proximity to the woman and the children, a husband and father. It is a 1990s 'lifestyle' commonplace that we are defined by the changing roles we play throughout our lives. Rielly's paintings explore the multiple construction of the self. His man and woman are in the process of inventing and assuming their identities. Each has the body of a young child and the head of an older adult, and they carry a 'prop' which stands for a stage in between. The props are clichés of aspiration - homeowner and bride. They also represent for Rielly the 'gap between where we are and where we want to be', the gap between desire and satisfaction in which most people hover.

These paintings are not portraits. *Man* and *Woman* are not individuals with abnormally small bodies, but are instead obvious composites. The artist has constructed them, as we construct ourselves, from many sources. He finds images in newspapers, books and magazines, then cuts them up and reassembles them. He projects the resulting collage onto canvas and paints the image produced. This process captures for the gallery the effect of disorientation produced by the sudden magnification of the image in the space of the studio. Rielly makes no attempts to conceal the disjunctions within his pictures: he makes an image which looks more like the head of a man stuck onto a representation of a little girl's dress than a man dressing up as a little girl.

Nevertheless, the images present a manipulated and fetishised identity. The young children, larger than life, have overtones of Lewis Carroll's *Alice in Wonderland*, of childish innocence observed and repackaged by adults. The simplicity of their presentation refers to the direct drawing style of children, but again it has been pushed towards something else. Both children have something 'wrong' with them, which the viewer may not immediately notice. The abnormality of the *Boy* seems something of a visual trick. His two pairs of arms cause the eye to flicker from one to the other, uncertain whether he really has two pairs of arms or

Facing page: *Man* 1995
Oil on canvas
1829 x 1524mm

Woman 1995
Oil on canvas
1829 x 1524mm

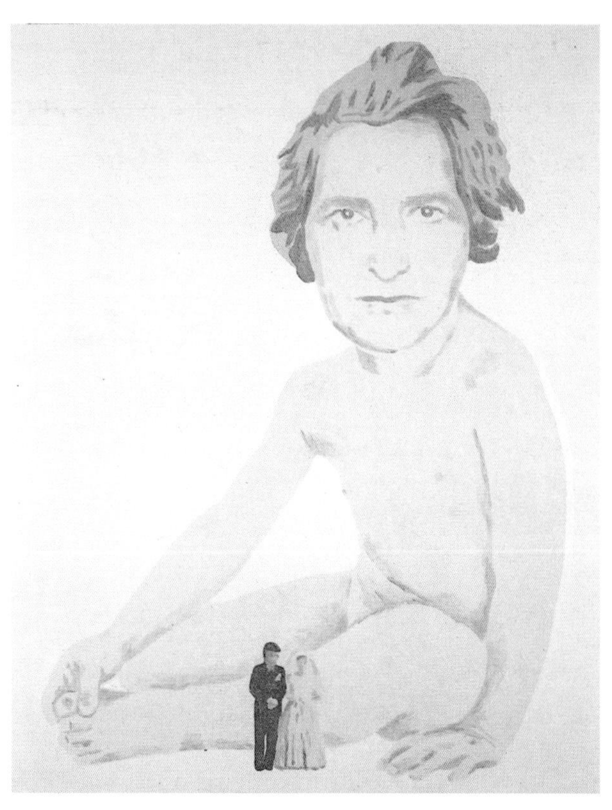

JAMES RIELLY

BIOGRAPHY

1956	Born in Wales
1974 - 1975	Deeside College, Wales
1975 - 1978	Gloucestershire College of Art and Design, Cheltenham
1980 - 1981	Belfast College of Art, Northern Ireland
1983 - 1984	Fellow at Artescape Trust, Lincoln
1984 - 1985	Fellow at The Fine Arts Work Centre, Provincetown, MA, USA
1988 - 1989	Fellow at Kunstlerhaus Bethanien, Berlin, Germany
1995	Momart Fellow at Tate Gallery Liverpool

Lives and works in London

SOLO EXHIBITIONS

1983	Art and Research Gallery, Belfast, Northern Ireland
1984	Hudson D Walker Gallery, Provincetown, MA, USA
1985	Hudson D Walker Gallery, Provincetown, MA, USA
	Bayer Gallery, Provincetown, MA, USA
1986	Carlile Gallery, London
1987	Carlile Gallery, London
1988	Alexander Roussos Gallery, London
1989	Kunstlerhaus Bethanien, Berlin
1990	Galerie Wittenbrink, Munich
1992	Galerie Wittenbrink, Munich
1993	Berning and Daw Fine Art, London
1994	Laurent Delaye, London
1995	Laurent Delaye, London

SELECTED GROUP EXHIBITIONS

1983	*Artescape Trust Exhibition*, Lincoln
	Douglas Hyde Gallery, Dublin, Southern Ireland
	New Heritage Exhibition - Welsh Arts Council, Oriel Gallery, Cardiff, Wales
	Brixton Art Gallery, London
1984	Hudson D Walker, Provincetown, MA, USA
	Ferens Art Gallery, Hull
	The Usher Gallery, Lincoln
	Blackfriars Art Gallery, Boston, UK
	Art Association Gallery and Museum, Provincetown, MA, USA
1985	*New Figurations*, Hudson D Walker Gallery, Princetown, MA, USA
	Bayer Gallery, Provincetown, MA, USA
	Recent Acquisitions Show, Art Association Gallery and Museum, Provincetown, MA, USA
1986	*Open Exhibition*, Riverside Studios, London
	Christopher Hull Gallery, London
	Groucho Club, London
1987	Christopher Hull Gallery, London
	Carlile Gallery, London
1989	Kunstlerhaus Bethanien, Berlin
1991	Britannia Works, London
1992	Connaught Brown Gallery, London
1993	*East*, Norwich Gallery, Norwich
1994	The Minories Art Gallery, Colchester
	Howard Gardens Gallery, Cardiff
	Flaxman Gallery, Stoke On Trent
	Fete Worse Than Death - Factual Nonsense, London
1995	Galerie Wittenbrink, Munich
	Making It: Process and Participation, Tate Gallery Liverpool

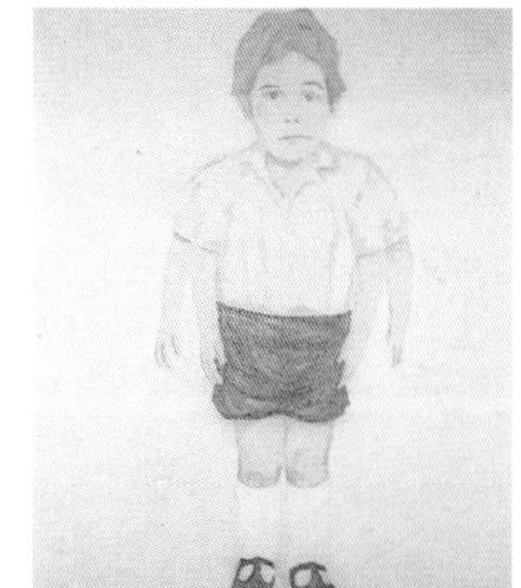

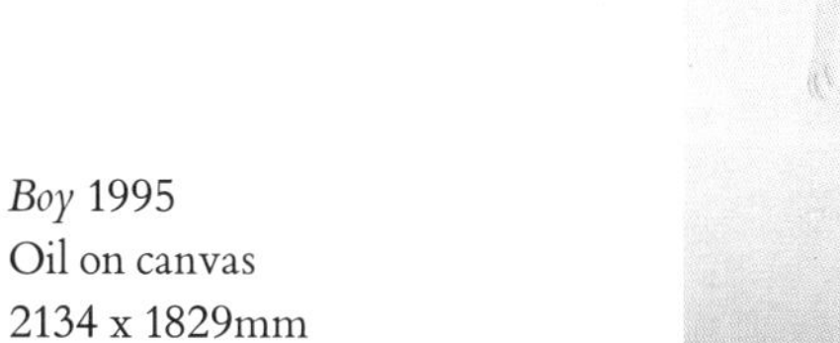

Boy 1995
Oil on canvas
2134 x 1829mm

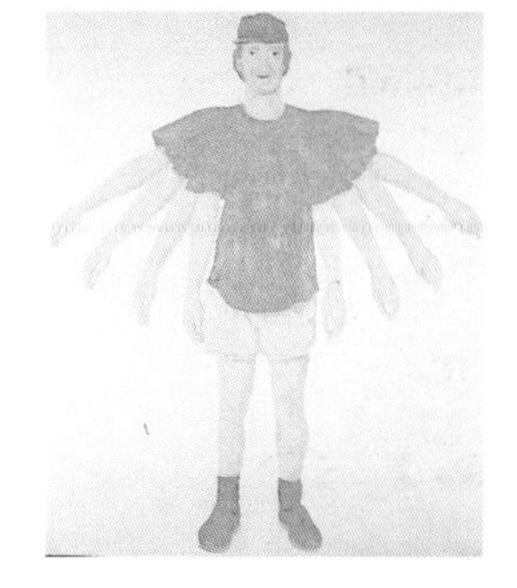

Young Man 1995
Oil on canvas
1829 x 1524mm

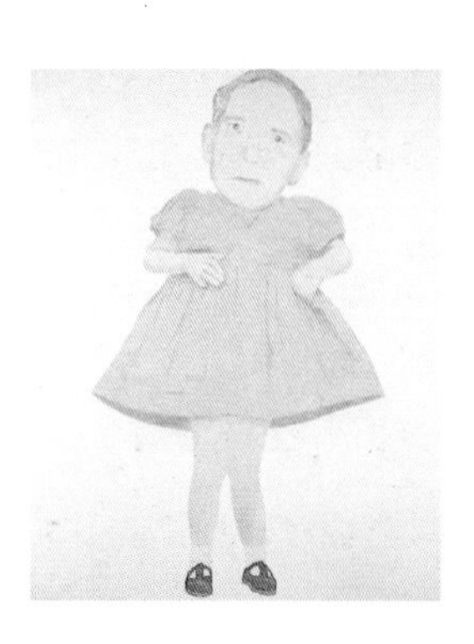

Older Man 1995
Oil on canvas
1829 x 1524mm

whether we are simply reading the image incorrectly.

The idea of a figure with more than one pair of arms is developed in the *Young Man*. Dressed in the same colours, this member of the family has eight arms. The multiplicity renders the abnormality more absurd but more explicable: the *Young Man* resembles gods of Indian religions such as the Hindu Shiva and Vishnu, who are often depicted with multiple arms to represent their power and cosmic omniscience. Rielly is a Buddhist, and Avalokiteshvara, a Buddhist archetype of compassion whose competence is expressed in an explosion of arms and heads, is also a source for his imagery. The multiple arms of Indian religious art was one of the main reasons why nineteenth-century European critics such as Ruskin found it barbaric. It was seen as an art which fractured rather than completed the body, alien to the standard conflation of beauty with truth. Rielly is clearly interested in the fracturing of the body, and the reference to Indian art in his work alters the status of that fracturing. What could at first only be read as deformity becomes desired difference, and the image retreats away from the actual back into the realm of representation.

Rielly's *Girl* embodies this intersection between the real and the pictorial. She and her cuddly toy both have three legs. The consistency of the abnormality brings it into question: what, in the world of this painting, constitutes normality? The painting challenges our perceptions of the normal and the abnormal, making it clear that this is an opposition constructed both relatively and artificially. If you were trying to help a child come to terms with difference, you might buy her a toy which looked like her.

This painting highlights the levels of visual acceptance which the others also explore. It is an amusing painting, but the humour it engenders is unsettling, as the viewer can never be entirely sure exactly what they are laughing at: the little girl, the style of her representation, or an imaginary three-legged universe. The comedy comes from the unexpected, but it hovers also around the unacceptable.

Ultimately, the worlds of the paintings are not real: they are realms of manipulated artificiality which enable us to reflect on the construction and representation of identity. They embody simultaneously both desire and disgust and invite us to consider them in relation to ourselves. The depicted bodies speak directly to our viewing bodies: we can map their similarities and their differences onto ourselves. Identity is essentially representational, and is about how to project and present the self to the outside world. It is reflective, as we receive our identities back from those inhabitants of the outside world for whom we project it. Rielly works with both the representational and the reflective aspects of identity, making figurative work which is almost as much about the needs, expectations and aspirations of the body of the viewer as it is about the bodies of the composite individuals it depicts.

James Rielly is Tate Gallery Liverpool's 1995 MOMART artist in residence.

Girl 1995
Oil on canvas
2134 x 1829mm

Padraig Timoney exhibits a group of works in which 'nothing is the same as anything else'. Conceived as a group, and made (with two exceptions) specifically for this exhibition, these paintings and objects engage the viewer in a series of visual exchanges. Much of their meaning resides in the nature of process; in the various processes they embody and in the tension they maintain between process and the processed, between process as a means of, and as a subject for art. The viewer's attention oscillates from what has been done and what there is still left to do: the artist is interested in a state of 'active looking'.

Timoney considers looking to be the counterpart of making, and to be similarly hard work. He seeks to make art which ensnares the viewer's visual imagination, triggering a mental process which runs parallel to the physical process which engendered the work. *An Ounce of Difference* flashes to attract our attention. A neon sign, it plays with the structuralist notion that all art works are texts or sequences of visual 'signs', and it confronts us with art which demands to be read. 'A half ounce' - 'half announce'. The two phrases are connected formally and conceptually: a half ounce is half an ounce, which is a homonymic pair for 'half announce'.

A homonym is an elaborate rhyme, and this implied homonym is reinforced by the actual rhyming of 'announce' with 'ounce'. This rhyme suggests a visual and aural correspondence between the two words. Once we notice this, we begin to understand the artist's reasons for combining the two phrases into this sign and, working backwards, we mirror the linguistic calculations which constituted its making.

Bad Reputations Start Fires relies on its gallery label to trap the viewer's visual imagination and identify it as 'art'. It is an ordinary fire extinguisher in a glass case, the label - 'fire extinguisher', dilute sulphuric acid, safety glass' alters its function and renders it potentially leathal. The glass case which seemed at first to prevent us accessing a safety device in the event of a disaster is in fact protecting us from one.

Timoney often uses language to control the tension between making and experiencing an artwork. He says that his oil painting, *Boss,* 'is about mastering or grasping something'. A hand grasps three rings from a gas cooker, and, in order to depict it, the artist masters a traditional painting technique, modelling form in careful modulations of dark and light tones. The viewer is invited to use the clue offered in the punning correspondence of motif and method to decipher or 'grasp' the painting's meaning. Timoney is interested in the way metaphors and other figures of speech encourage a comparative type of looking which heightens understanding while at the same time necessitating a conceptual detour. He likes to literalise language, hence his word play in *Boss* and his recent paintings made with rabbit skin glue, a substance more commonly used only to prime a canvas prior to painting. In these works he is seeking a *tabula rasa*, returning painting literally to its origins by making finished, gestural pictures out of something generally used as a 'primer'.

Much of the artist's use of language involves humour, and both comedy and irony punctuate his work. *A Joppic Faq* is a nonsense title intended to imply 'something that came from Joppa'. The work is a spray painting made on a section of plaster removed from the wall of a house which was going to be demolished when the artist moved out. The artist sees it in relation to *Fungus Rules the Brazen Cars:* it is a representation *on* rather than *of* architecture, a piece of visual vandalism which has become an artwork.

Fungus Rules the Brazen Cars makes ironic reference to WB Yeats' *Who Goes With Fergus,*and its plaster mushrooms

Facing Page: *Knife of Fork* 1995
Fork and slide
260 x 25 x 15mm

A Joppic Fag 1992
Spray paint on
plaster in
cement, wood
960 x 1000mm

PADRAIG TIMONEY

BIOGRAPHY

1968	Born in Derry, Northern Ireland
1987	St Martins School of Art
1988	Goldsmiths College
1991	Nicholas and Andrei Toot Travelling Scholarship

Lives and works in Liverpool

SOLO EXHIBITIONS

1992	Golsmiths Gallery, London
	Milch Gallery, London
1993	*September*, Laure Genillard Gallery, London
1994	Galleria Raucci/Santamaria, Napoli

GROUP EXHIBITIONS

1991	*Damien Duffy and Padraig Timoney*, Bridge Gallery, London
	Four Sculptors: Martin Creed, Jim Hamlyn, Angela Peers, Padraig Timoney, Laure Genillard Gallery, London
1992	*Love at First Sight*, The Showroom, London
	Hit and Run, 50 Tufton Street, London
1993	*East*, Norwich Gallery, Norwich
	Escale-Stopover-Tussenstop, Musee d'Art Moderne, Villeneuve d'Ascq, France
1994	*Group show*, Laure Genillard Gallery, London
	Galerie Martina Detterer, Frankfurt
	Drawings, Laure Genillard Gallery, London
	Words are Deeds, Alessandra Bonomo Gallery, Rome
	Rien à Signaler, Analix, Geneva
	My Car Is Black And Yours Is White, Galerie Mladych, Mesta Brno Hungary
	Laure Genillard Gallery, London
1995	*Making It: Process and Participation*, Tate Gallery Liverpool
	Wild Roses Grow By The Roadside, 152c Brick Lane, London
	Nakr Hrane, Galerie Vaclav, Spaly, Prague

Not illustrated:
Mad Repeater (diptych)
1995
Rabbit skin glue, indian
ink on canvas/wooden
frame on paper
750 x 655 x 45mm
665 x 560 x 70mm

Skull+Bones (diptych)
1995
Rabbit skin glue,
indian ink on
canvas/wooden
frame on paper
500 x 625 x 45mm

Herrschaft 1995
Acrylic paint on plaster
720 x 540mm

Boss 1995
Oil on canvas
1620 x 2135mm

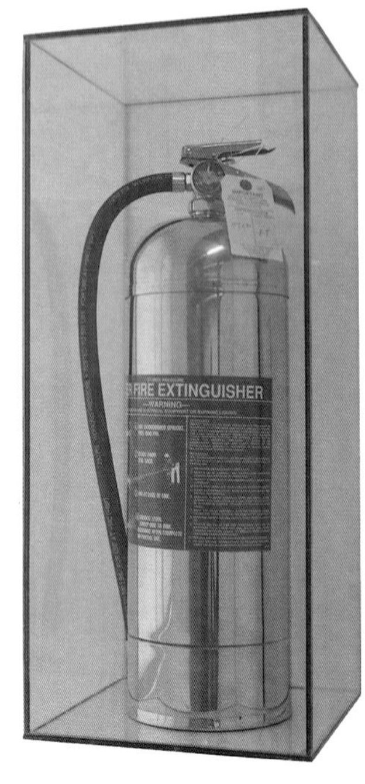

Bad Reputations Start Fires 1995
Fire extinguisher, sulphuric acid, safety glass
700 x 300 x 300mm

are again the literalisation of a mode of speech . Part of Yeats' poem reads:

'For Fergus rules the brazen cars
And rules the shadows of the wood
And the white breast of the dim sea
And all dishevelled wandering stars'

Timoney turns the 'dishevelled wandering stars' into satellite dishes which spring up overnight in streets and on housing estates like mushrooms. The artist suggests that they are a creeping fungus. The mushrooms also tell a joke: mushrooms can be hallucinogenic. Like television, they can make you see brightly coloured images which are not really there. The mushrooms also serve a pictorial function, and perhaps the puns and jokes, for which they are a vehicle, help a viewer look at them for long enough to work this out. They follow the laws of perspective - those on houses in the background are tiny, those in the foreground much larger. They offer an alternative formal system by which to decipher the space of the painting.

Ultimately, Timoney's works play games with the viewer. They give us clues, and demand the kind of active looking which results not in resolution but continued oscillation between making and meaning. *Knife of Fork* sits on a plinth at table height, inviting us to pick it up and try to use it. The plinth fends us off, but so also does the object itself: it is actively dysfunctional. The fork has been transformed into a knife by the addition of exposed slide film in the shape of a blade. The film is too dark to be used, the knife too insubstantial. We can see how it was made, and by looking, reconstruct the process, but the object still has us trapped in the circularity of its meaning.

An Ounce of Difference was made possible by support from Benson Signs

Fungus Rules the Brazen Cars 1995
Oil paint and plaster on canvas,
1836 x 3660 x 50mm

An Ounce of Difference 1995
Neon sign in Perspex case
500 x 3000 x 200mm

Lot's Wife is a pear tree hedge made from tin foil and wire. From above, speakers transmit the recorded voice of an old man insisting on the gullability of his audience: 'Ah you're an April Fool'. For giving this art work our attention? For suspending disbelief for a moment and thinking that these enchanted trees are speaking to us?

The hedge is not tidy. It looks like a hedge which has grown out of control, straggling and unkempt although once carefully cultivated. In making it, Daphne Wright was thinking of hedges she has seen on old farms in Ireland, laid by families putting down roots and establishing boundaries in a new place. The hedge is like something one might come upon in a forgotten garden, abandoned and over-grown but still needlessly producing fruit, a remnant of someone's desire to stamp their ownership on nature and on the land. The artist comes from Ireland, and her family home is a farm. She has been living in England for six years now, a rural person dwelling in cities, and the tension between the rural and the urban in her own experience impregnates her work. She notices parks, allotments, gardens; the 'snippets' of countryside which serve only to remind you that you are in a city.

In the Bible story, Lot's wife was turned into a pillar of salt because she looked back at her native land as it was being destroyed by God's wrath. Wright's hedge is primarily about looking back - into Irish and personal history. The voice is the voice of the artist's father. She wanted it to sound rough, old and intrinsically rural, in contrast to the rather high, bright and clear 'voice' the tinfoil trees might be expected to have.

As well as real memories, memories of fables run throughout this work. The artist has turned fruit trees into metal, echoing the transformation of Lot's wife and linking the work to other stories of metamorphosis. In Greek mythology, mortals are often transformed into trees, stars or other elements from the natural world, for their protection or punishment. The metallic artificiality of the tin foil makes the trees of the hedge look like part of an enchanted forest, faintly echoing the forest in *The Sleeping Beauty*, *The Singing Ringing Tree* and the silver nutmeg and golden pear of *The Little Nut Tree*. The trees look frozen or petrified into unnatural and premature winter - the winter enforced by Persephone's annual six-monthly exile in the Underworld or that caused by Oscar Wilde's *The Selfish Giant*'s refusal to allow children to enjoy his garden.

Enchanted forests and human trees are not real, and *Lot's Wife* is primarily concerned with artifice. The brilliant artificiality of the tinfoil mocks the still fertile, abundant shape of the pears: the work is more about mimicry than mimesis. One of Wright's sources for the image of the trees is the work of Giotto, who, in frescoes such as *The Miracle of the Spring*, uses stylised trees, springing uselessly out of bare rock, to signal the order of the miraculous. Wright's tinfoil pear trees represent trees which are, in Ireland, already artificially transplanted and out of place. Here they are reproduced in a fake material and an unnatural space, at several removes from any notion of a 'natural' pear tree. So also with the 'voice' of the trees: its theatricality builds transparency and artifice into the very process of the supposedly mimetic endeavour of making a tree from foil.

Lot's Wife 1995
Tinfoil, wire
and cement
2230 x 11080 x 1680mm

DAPHNE WRIGHT

BIOGRAPHY

1963	Born in Ireland
1981 - 1985	Sligo Regional Technical College
1985 - 1987	Dublin National College of Art & Design
1989 - 1991	Newcastle-upon-Tyne Polytechnic
1991 - 1992	Awarded Cheltenham Fellowship
1992 - 1993	British - Rome Scholarship in Sculpture
1993 - 1994	'Diaspora' Project, commission from Living Arts Project (funded by Irish Arts Council) Manchester Metropolitan University Fellowship (funded by Henry Moore Foundation)

SOLO EXHIBITIONS

1994	Cornerhouse, Manchester
	The Model Arts Centre, Sligo, Ireland
	Limerick City Centre Art Gallery, Ireland
	Domestic Shrubbery (one-person travelling show)
1995	*Domestic Shrubbery*, Castlefield, Manchester

GROUP EXHIBITIONS

1985	Temple Bar Diploma Show, Dublin
	Yeats Gallery, Sligo
1986	*Sculpture in Context,* Dublin
	Miniature Art, Del Bello Gallery, Toronto
1988	Sculpture Open Exhibition, RHA
	Gallagher Gallery, Dublin
1989	W B Yeats Summer School Symposium & Exhibition (funded by Sculpture Society), Sligo
1990	Irish Life Graduate Show, Dublin
	The Arts Festival, Sligo
1991	The Gymnasium, Goldsmiths, London
1992	Cheltenham Fellow Show, Pittville Gallery, Cheltenham
1993	*Full Circle*, British School at Rome, Italy
	Arte e Altro Giovani Artisti 5, Rome
	Territoria, Sala I, Rome
1995	*Clot*, Artforms, London
	Making It: Process and Participation
	Tate Gallery Liverpool

The deliberate artificiality of *Lot's Wife* pits nature against culture. Does culture win? Perhaps not - the straggling hedge suggests the power of nature to revert to wildness after man's interventions have ceased, and the mocking voice insists that the viewer is not completely in control of the work's signifying processes. Perhaps there is a natural reality hidden in the tinfoil of the hedge: metamorphosis is a process of embodiment as much as of disembodiment. Lot's Wife may have remained inside her pillar of salt, and how do we know that there are not real pears imprisoned in the tinfoil?

The Biblical and mythological references buried within the work invite us to think about what exactly it is that we, as viewers, believe. What are the roots that we cannot deny? Turning or looking back to those roots often implies their absence and the presence instead of a trick or calamitous practical joke - Lot's wife, Orpheus and Euridice, even the childhood game of Grandmother's Footsteps, where the action of looking back is accompanied by the faint dread of being sneaked up on. Ultimately, *Lot's Wife* plays a trick on the viewer. The trees are not going to awaken; the voice can only mock, can only sing one, base and vulgar song.

Lot's Wife is supported by Bacofoil

The artist would also like to thank Shirley MacWilliam for her help with the installation.

Looking Both Ways is a visual and spatial re-enactment of an investigation into Liverpool's Royal Liver Building which Those Environmental Artists (TEA) have been conducting for the last nine months. Process does not so much inform the work as become embodied within it. Essentially concerned with intervention, if not subversion, the four artists who together make up the collective TEA have since 1987 been working together to set up what they call 'temporary institutions' to make art works. Their art looks at the forms and formalities of historical, cultural, factual and conceptual commodities. It is the setting up of the 'institution' which defines the appearance and content of the art work.

Invited to make a work for Tate Gallery Liverpool, TEA identified the Royal Liver Building as a building which occupies an important place in the mythologies of the city. Visible from the Gallery, the Liver Building is as symbolic of Liverpool as the Eiffel Tower is of Paris: if the focus of a news story or TV drama moves to Liverpool, the camera will inevitably show the building. Because of its unique status, TEA decided to make the Liver Building the centre of this project.

TEA approached the Liver Building, as we all do, from the outside. They collected postcards, views and sightings of the building from all over town. One of these was sent to Royal Liver Assurance and its tenant companies to ask if they would participate in the project by showing TEA something of the inner life of the building. A display was set up to attract the interest of employees from the various companies, and to encourage them to contribute their 'inside stories' of the building to TEA. They did this on a questionnaire in the form of a postcard showing the view of the Liver Building from the Tate. TEA identified individuals willing to share their impressions of their own corner of the building, and the artists interviewed and recorded these individuals, photographing the space that typified the building for them.

The experiences of individual employees in the Liver Building presented TEA with a different view of the landmark - from the inside out - to complement the ones they already had. This new, composite view forms the basis for their continuing investigation into the building's domination of the city. This investigation is now presented in the installation *Looking Both Ways*. In the gallery, members of the public are invited to complete a questionnaire, contributing their response to the Liver Building as seen from the gallery, to the revelations of the employees, and to other buildings which have a similar symbolic power. The form of the installation, continually revised and extended as it is, mirrors the process of the 'temporary institution' which instigated it. The first room presents an initial view of the building, from the outside. The window shows the actual view, reflected and deflected in the multiple postcards and images of the building used in corporate literature. TV monitors showing the opening sequences of *The Liver Birds* and *Brookside* demonstrate the consistent power of the Liver Building to represent Liverpool across several decades of shifting taste and style.

Moving from this room into the next, the viewer is confronted by a wall of the questionnaires completed by Liver Building employees. To read them, you have to go round the other side - look both ways - and again the

BIOGRAPHIES

Jon Biddulph

1958	Born in Congleton, Cheshire
1976 - 1977	Manchester Polytechnic
1977 - 1980	Studied Three Dimensional Design, Manchester Polytechnic
1980 - 1981	Ceramics Fellow, University of Salford

Lives and works in Manchester

Peter Hatton

1956	Born in Rossendale, Lancashire
1974 - 1975	Rochdale College of Art
1975 - 1978	Liverpool Polytechnic

Lives and works in London

Val Murray

1944	Born in Edinburgh
1979 - 1980	Stockport College of Technology
1980 - 1984	Manchester Polytechnic

Lives and works in Manchester

Lynn Pilling

1960	Born in Bolton, Lancashire
1979	Mid Warwickshire College of Further Education, Leamington Spa
1980 - 1983	Manchester Polytechnic
1985 - 1986	Hertfordshire College of Art and Design, St Albans

Lives and works in Manchester

PROJECTS AS TEA

1987	*Homeworks*: an exploration of the layered history of a semi-derelict house in a still lived-in street in Levenshulme, Manchester.
1988	*If Only Walls Could Speak*: an examination of heritage by re-presenting aspects of Wythenshawe Hall, Manchester *Baggages*: the components of a home carried through the streets, assembled and supported by its occupants
1989	*In Transit*: contents of suitcases revealed at bus stations
1990	*In Situ*: the identification, labelling and display of ordinary objects in the Flag Market, Preston
1991	*Living Space Series:* an investigation into the role of ordinary objects in relation to the spaces we and they occupy: Stoke on Trent - full - sized ceramic house. Light, sound, projections. Liverpool - versions of domestic furniture in different media and formats in four city centre sites. Manchester - residency in former Victorian Market Hall to construct giant garments from ordinary garments. Night event - sound, light, music
1993-94	*Other Peoples Shoes*: collaborative investigation into shoes. In six stages. In clubs, shops, a factory and galleries. With Impossible Theatre
1994	*Anxiety and Escapism*: part of the Milennium Festival at the Royal Festival Hall, London. An investigation into people's perception of the 1930s
1994 -95	*Looking Both Ways*: an investigation of the Liver Building - from civic symbol to work place. With Tate Gallery Liverpool
1995	*Orleans House*: research for project to re-evaluate the site of a stately home

Looking Both Ways 1995
Mixed media installation

physical matches the intellectual. In the centre of the room are ten spaces in which the viewer may experience a variety of individual views of the Liver Building. Each space contains three images of one of these views and a telephone on which you can listen to a personal account of it. They are surrounded by other alternative ways of describing the building: TEA have collected architectural plans, maps of the heating and wiring systems, specifications for the boiler. The emphasis on planning and mapping reinforces TEA's project of re-mapping the Liver Building.

Much of this re-mapping has to do with the positioning of the individual and the private alongside or inside the corporate and the public. The individual spaces in the second room of the installation are enclosed in a growing wall of postcards - the questionnaires completed by visitors to the installation. These questionnaires provide a forum for the voice of the individual. The installation functions on a one-to-one basis: the viewer reads the questionnaires, listens to the recordings and may respond. It is in this way, perhaps, that TEA's activity may be looked at as subversive: in highlighting the individual they turn buildings inside out, making them collections of individuals, audiences and participants. Their installation, hugely ambitious in scope, is intimate in presentation. Manifesting a series of points of view, it offers an insight into the functioning of a building and, beyond that perhaps, into the definition of a city.

Looking Both Ways is sponsored by Royal Liver Assurance.

TEA also thank Philip Alcock, Rebekah Ayres, Glyn Morris, the companies and contractors in the Royal Liver Building, Mersey TV Co. Ltd, Arup Associates, Kingham Knight Associates, British Telecom, and everyone who made a sound recording or filled in a questionnaire.